FAQ

TEEN LIFE™

FREQUENTLY ASKED QUESTIONS ABOUT

College and
Career Training

Jason
Porterfield

ROSEN
PUBLISHING®

New York

Published in 2009 by The Rosen Publishing Group, Inc.
29 East 21st Street, New York, NY 10010

Library of Congress Cataloging-in-Publication Data

Porterfield, Jason.
Frequently asked questions about college and career training / Jason Porterfield.
    p.cm.—(FAQ: teen life)
Includes index.
ISBN-13: 978-1-4042-1803-1 (library binding)
1. College applications—United States. 2. College choice—United States. 3. Vocational guidance—United States. I. Title.
LB2351.52.U6P67 2009
378.1'61—dc22

                                        2008000001

Manufactured in the United States of America

Contents

Chapter one

WHAT ARE SOME HIGHER EDUCATION OPTIONS?

Students graduating from high school have a wide variety of options to consider for continuing their education. Most students regard college study as the next logical step toward building the foundation for a successful career, but there are a number of other post–high school programs worthy of investigation. If you decide against attending college, you may want to look into options such as agricultural schools, culinary institutes, art schools, trade schools, and vocational programs. Another option may be to consider pursuing a career with the U.S. military.

Whether you attend college or pursue another form of post–high school program, you will have a wide variety of factors to consider, from size to academic focus, when planning your education. Some institutions are large universities with tens of thousands of students. Others may have fewer than a thousand students enrolled.

The majority of students may live in dorms located on the campus, or most may commute in from their off-campus homes.

One significant difference is between private and state colleges. State colleges are funded by the state budget and by taxpayers, though they also receive some funding from private individuals and groups. Private colleges are operated as corporate entities using funds given by private citizens and organizations, and they do not receive any state funding. Private colleges are often more expensive than state schools but may have more latitude regarding what they teach because they don't depend on state funding.

Another fundamental difference is that between colleges and universities. A college offers a selection of degrees from one core area, such as business or the liberal arts. Universities are large schools that actually combine several different schools. A university may have a school of medicine, a business school, an art school, and so on.

Many colleges have an area of specialization, such as art, music, agriculture, or business. Culinary schools focus on subjects related to cooking professionally, while film schools cover subjects related to filmmaking. Look for colleges that have strong programs in the area you're interested in. Also consider the school's reputation for excellence. Will classes be challenging enough for you? In many cases, a "B" average and a demanding course load at an upper-tier college will carry as much or more weight than an "A" at a school with lower standards. So, even if you will have to work harder to keep up with your classes, it may be worthwhile to choose a more academically demanding college.

Columbia University is a large school whose main campus is on 116th Street and Broadway in New York City. Prospective students can learn about Columbia's programs and the city's cultural offerings at the Visitor's Center and in a tour of the various campuses.

Location

Another factor that may influence your choice of schools is the campus location. Is the school in a city, a town, or a rural setting? What's the topography like? How is the weather? Relocating to a completely different setting can be an adventure, but think carefully about the consequences before doing so. A school's location could have a greater impact on your education than you may think. You'll have to decide which setting would be the most comfortable learning environment for you and whether you

The University of Utah, in Salt Lake City, is situated in a valley of the Wasatch Mountains. The mountains can offer students recreational activities such as hiking and mountain biking in the summer and skiing in the winter.

can adapt to new surroundings. If you come from a large city, for example, and enroll in a small institution in a rural area, you may have difficulty adjusting to the relative quiet and open landscape. The reverse can be true for students from a small town enrolling in a city college.

You should also think about how far from home you're willing to go for college. The perfect school for you may be on the other side of the country, or just across town. Consider how often you'll want to return home. If you think that you'd like to see your family and friends every weekend, you'll probably want to stay within a short drive from home. If you're fine with seeing them only over long breaks and holidays, think about looking at schools several hours away. If you do decide to attend a college far away from home, you'll want to think about how you'll get your stuff to your school. Will you have a car, or will your parents drive you? Will you take a plane, train, or bus home for breaks?

Size

You'll want to consider the size of the campus and its layout. Are buildings close together, or is the campus spread out? Is it close to town? Take into account the number of students who are enrolled. There are advantages to both large schools and small schools. Large schools often have a more varied student body and may offer more extracurricular activities. They will likely be more familiar to future employers. Their size and resources, coupled with a good academic reputation, may help attract top-notch faculty. At smaller schools, there will likely be a lower ratio of students to professors, meaning that students receive a fair amount of individual attention from faculty and staff. A smaller school may not have an easily recognizable name, but it may compensate with a reputation for highly selective admissions standards.

Both kinds of schools also have disadvantages. Larger colleges with tens of thousands of students can seem overwhelmingly crowded and make students feel isolated. At universities, it is not unusual for one college to completely overshadow the others, making faculty and students feel neglected. Classes can be too

At small colleges, the class sizes can be smaller and, therefore, more personal and friendly than those offered at large universities. At larger schools, some classes might often be held in auditoriums and lecture halls.

large for professors to get to know individual students and give them the attention they deserve. Some lecture classes may even be conducted by graduate students. Smaller schools, where everyone seems to know everyone else, can feel claustrophobic. Shy students may feel intimidated in small classes where everyone else seems to be asking questions or offering opinions.

You may also think about the extracurricular activities available. If you're athletic, you might want to find out more about the school's sports programs. If you enjoy theater or the performing arts, look at schools that have strong theater or music programs.

If you're interested in joining a fraternity or sorority, you may rule out schools that don't have a Greek system.

Four-Year or Two-Year?

You will also want to decide whether to attend a two-year or four-year school. Two-year colleges are often known as junior colleges or community colleges. Where four-year colleges offer bachelor's degrees, two-year schools give associate's degrees upon completion of course work. Many four-year colleges will accept college credits earned at a two-year college and will apply them to a four-year field of study. Like four-year colleges, two-year colleges have areas of specialization, many oriented toward setting students up for rapid entry into their chosen profession.

Two-year colleges are generally commuter schools, meaning that the majority of students live off campus, though there are often exceptions for particularly intense programs such as culinary schools. Two-year colleges are often easier to get into than four-year colleges, but their class schedules and workloads are still demanding. You'll likely have to work just as hard and spend as much time studying as you would in a four-year program.

part two

HOW DO YOU GATHER INFORMATION/ RESEARCH?

Finding information on colleges and other post–high school educational programs is relatively easy. Many prospective students begin receiving college brochures during their sophomore or junior year of high school. By the time you're ready to decide where you want to apply, you'll likely have dozens of brochures and course catalogs on hand.

You'll probably also want to look around for information on colleges, rather than simply waiting for schools to contact you. Many magazines run annual feature stories that rank individual colleges, so you may want to keep an eye out for those issues. Don't focus strictly on schools that appear in these rankings, though. Many excellent schools never make it onto these lists—especially smaller, specialized institutions—though they may have strong programs and good reputations.

You can find information on colleges through your guidance counselor or by going online. Most colleges have Web sites where you can find an overview of the curriculum and requirements. Your guidance counselor will probably have many resources on hand, such as course catalogs and contact information for many colleges. He or she will also have pamphlets and flyers on a variety of other educational programs.

Brochures and Mailings

Colleges of all sizes mail information to thousands of students each year. Even the smallest schools send out many times

more mailers than there are students in each incoming class. By mailing information to so many potential students, colleges hope to attract a large enough percentage of applicants so that they can be selective in admitting incoming students. Colleges typically send out mailers to

Colleges usually send brochures and information packets to prospective students during the junior year in high school. The materials feature the basic information about the respective college, including its history, courses of study, and admissions procedures.

students based on answers from questionnaires given along with standardized tests such as the SAT and ACT. You can also have yourself added to a school's mailing list by directly requesting information.

Many college mailers are simple brochures. They often feature images of the campus and students, as well as a short history of the school. They'll probably list a few basic facts, like the average annual cost of attendance, the number of students in the school, and the courses of study available. They also include contact information, such as the address and telephone number of the school's office of admissions, as well as the address for the college's Web site. More elaborate mailers feature magazine-sized brochures and may include a blank application form. Some schools may send out course catalogs, student publications, or even videos intended to give prospective students a glimpse of student life on their campus.

College Fairs and Recruiters

There may also be college fairs held in your area. College fairs usually feature recruiters from dozens of local and regional colleges, as well as other educational programs. College fairs offer excellent opportunities for prospective applicants to speak face-to-face with representatives from multiple schools in one place. These recruiters set up tables or booths and offer information about the schools they represent, taking questions from prospective students and handing out brochures. They often offer the opportunity to be put on their mailing list so that you

This recruiter from the University of Florida explains some of the offerings of the school and campus to prospective students who are attending a college fair.

can receive more information in the future. The fairs are generally free and open to students from many nearby high schools. High schools usually provide transportation to college fairs for students in the eleventh and twelfth grades.

It's also not unusual for college recruiters to come directly to high schools and distribute information. With the school administration's permission, they generally make themselves available to talk to students and answer questions in a common area during lunch.

Sorting Information

Once you have your information, you'll need to come up with a system for sorting through it. Make a checklist of what you want in a school. What field of study are you interested in? Are you looking for a program close to home or far away? Think about the impression that school representatives made on you. Were they helpful, or did they have trouble answering your questions satisfactorily? You'll likely want to factor in each school's cost, as well as any scholarships it offers.

Consider what kind of career you'd like to have and what sort of education you need to prepare yourself. Factor in the income you would likely have and whether or not the field would hold your interest. Consider a couple of areas of interest in the event that you change your mind about one.

Once you have some goal in mind, contact schools that are strong in the area you're interested in. Many colleges will arrange for you to talk to faculty, students, or alumni involved with your prospective field of study who can tell you about the program and answer your questions.

Seeing the Campus

You may also want to arrange a visit to the campus to see what the school is like for yourself before deciding to apply. Making a visit can significantly influence your decision regarding whether or not to apply to a particular college. There is no better way to find out what a campus is like and how a school is run. Many

When you do research on a college, make a checklist of what you want in a school. For instance, does the school have a respected library? Are the campus grounds safe and pleasant?

school admissions offices run tours throughout the week for prospective students, especially during the spring when students are making their final decisions. Some schools even invite prospective students to stay overnight with a "dorm host," a student who shows them what daily life on the campus is like.

When you visit a campus, pay attention to the school's layout and grounds. Take a tour and see the library, dorms, and academic buildings. If possible, eat a meal in the dining hall. Make notes of your observations and use them when you make your final decision about where you want to apply. A college's landscaping or the quality of its food may seem inconsequential when you're looking at a brochure. Experiencing them firsthand, however, contributes to a generally favorable or unfavorable impression of the institution that will influence your final decision.

When you contact schools, make sure to get any information you can on grants or scholarships that they may offer. If you visit a school, drop by its financial aid office. The staff may be able to tell you about available awards and the sort of work you need to do to receive them. Find out whether the school's scholarships or awards call for essays or letters of recommendation, and have those lined up before the application deadline.

Do some research on other forms of financial aid offered by the school, such as work-study programs or departmental awards. Most schools offer work-study awards in a variety of departments and positions, from dining halls to libraries. Some schools have a hierarchical work-study system, where new award recipients are required to work in the dining halls before taking a job in another department. Other schools allow students to apply for any available work-study job at the college.

Myths and Facts

I don't think I can go to college because I am not sure about where I want to go or how to apply.

Fact ➡ Approach your school guidance counselor for help in researching colleges and obtaining application information. Attend college fairs in your region and talk to people you know who have gone to a university. Check out various college Web sites to learn more about campuses, student life, and application requirements.

If I go to college, I'll have to go to one far away.

Fact ➡ You don't have to go to a college that is located far away from your home. Some students prefer to go away to college, but others stay near their home for various reasons, including financial or family reasons.

I can't go to college because I can't afford it.

Fact ➡ Some public colleges are quite affordable. It is not impossible to go to college.

Many colleges have financial aid opportunities available, such as academic scholarships, work-study jobs, and various student loans. Another choice might be to attend a community college for a year and then transfer to a university later, to save money. Another option is to attend a college that you can commute to instead of living on campus.

If I spend thousands of dollars on a four-year college, I'll never be able to earn enough money to pay off my tuition debt after I've graduated.

Fact ➡ Although the average gap in earnings between people with bachelor's degrees and those with only a high school diploma has narrowed, according the Census Bureau, college grads make nearly twice as much as high school graduates. Having a college education can provide more job opportunities than having only a high school diploma.

WHAT ARE INTERNSHIPS AND APPRENTICESHIPS?

If you have a career in mind, one way to make sure it's right for you is to serve an apprenticeship or do an internship in a related field. Internships and apprenticeships are very similar to each other, though apprenticeships often last longer than internships and are oriented more toward directing the apprentice into a specific job. Internships, on the other hand, usually cover a broader range of work experiences and give a more general overview of a career field. An internship applies your training and education to a real-world work situation, complementing your education by thrusting you into an entry-level position in your field of interest.

It is not uncommon for colleges or other educational programs to require that students complete internships. High school students may want to consider a school's internship opportunities when weighing it against others.

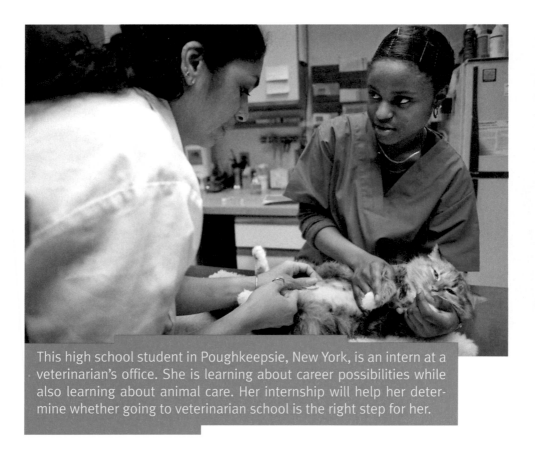

This high school student in Poughkeepsie, New York, is an intern at a veterinarian's office. She is learning about career possibilities while also learning about animal care. Her internship will help her determine whether going to veterinarian school is the right step for her.

Elite colleges may have ties to corporations that recruit interns from that institution. Specialized schools may have connections with businesses related to their field. The Culinary Institute of America, for example, incorporates into its curricula an eighteen-week "externship" opportunity at an approved restaurant or other establishment.

Apprenticeships and internships are mutually beneficial relationships. The intern or apprentice works for a company or individual for generally low wages in return for learning about the job or business for a specified period of time.

Workplace Experiences

Within companies that offer internships, the interns are usually seen as the lowest rung of the employment ladder. They often carry out tasks that the regular employees are too busy to perform, such as running errands, doing research, filing, and making coffee. Even if you are officially attached to a particular office or branch of a company, you may find yourself shuffled back and forth between departments as your help is needed.

Work hours for interns vary among employers. An after-school internship may only require an hour or two of your time each afternoon. A summer-long internship is likely to require forty hours a week, a typical workweek for many regular workers. Intense, short-term internships designed to fully immerse you in a business may require even more of your time. Be cautious of such internships, as the company may be looking for low-wage employees to exploit. Before beginning an internship, make sure that your hours and compensation are clearly stated and that they are satisfactory to you.

As you serve your internship, take your low status and shifting responsibilities in stride. Remember that you're there to learn, and seize the opportunity to find out as much about your duties, the various departments, the company, and even its employees as you can. Show enthusiasm for the work and do what you can to impress your employers. Demonstrating a quick grasp of the company's inner workings and an eye for details will show the company that you have a feel for the work, which may earn you a job or reference in the future.

At career fairs, many high school students have the opportunity to speak with college and employer representatives about the various internships that are available to them.

Internship Benefits

Internships and apprenticeships rarely pay much, if at all, and the work often appears menial or boring. However, the experience they offer can be invaluable. By doing an internship, you will learn how the business is structured and run, as well as become familiar with its daily routine. Learning all aspects of a company's organization can be beneficial as you decide what kind of career you want. You may begin an internship with a particular job as your ultimate goal. As you serve your internship, you may discover another aspect of the same field that interests you more than your original goal.

Serving an internship is also a good way to enhance your college applications. Many guidance counselors recommend that high school students do an internship, if possible. Internships are by no means required for applying to college, but serving one related to your stated field of interest will show admissions officials that you're truly interested in pursuing that field, and that you've already gained firsthand experience in the workplace.

Internships and apprenticeships are excellent ways to make connections in a particular field or even find a job for the future. If you impress your supervisors, they may be willing to write a letter of recommendation for you or perhaps offer you a future job with the company. Even if you have a negative experience, you will have learned from it and perhaps pursue another career.

Internships and apprenticeships are available with a wide variety of businesses or organizations, including large corporations, small businesses, nonprofit organizations, and government agencies. High school guidance counselors are usually the best people to ask about finding an internship. They can help you decide what kind of company or organization you want to work for, as well as what kind of work you want to do and how it may benefit you in the future. They may also be able to provide you with contact information. If you already know what kind of internship you want, you can contact companies and organizations on your own.

A teen volunteer explains the habitat of a horseshoe crab to a young visitor at a living museum in Virginia. Listing any community service and volunteer work that you've done in high school will improve the attractiveness of your college application.

Community Service

Any college application is enhanced by community service, which demonstrates to admissions officials that you're interested in the world around you as well as in your grades and school activities. Museums, libraries, churches, hospitals, schools, and many other organizations and institutions are happy to have volunteers contribute their time and energy. As with an internship, serving as a volunteer can help you figure out whether you want to pursue a particular career by exposing you to entry-level tasks. You'll also learn about the organization's structure, departments, and leadership.

Before you become a volunteer, consider what kind of work you want to do. If you're interested in becoming a librarian, you may try volunteering to reshelve books at your local branch library. Or, if you think you want to work with animals, sign up to walk dogs at an animal shelter. Whatever you choose to do, make sure you have the time and energy to follow through without neglecting your studies and still do a good job. Excellent letters of recommendation and even future jobs can result from performing your volunteer duties conscientiously and well. Also remember that volunteer work is unpaid, its reward being the knowledge that you've contributed to the well-being of your community.

four

HOW DO YOU DECIDE WHERE TO APPLY?

Once you've gotten information from schools and researched various programs, you'll have to begin deciding which schools to apply to and how many applications you want to send in. At this stage, you likely have a good idea of what you want in a school, as well as reasonable expectations about where you can apply based on factors such as cost, geography, and your grades and test scores. Even so, narrowing your list of schools down to a relative handful can be frustrating. Don't be afraid to ask your parents, your teachers, your guidance counselor, and your friends for advice. They may have insights into a particular school that you missed. Perhaps a friend has a sibling who attends a college you are interested in and you can ask that person about the school. Also remember that you can always call or e-mail schools if you have questions.

Try to review all the admissions information about a college that your guidance counselor or school library provides. Go over your research and look at your possibilities and choices carefully.

Reviewing Your Options

Narrowing your choices down from dozens of schools to a handful can seem like an enormous job. If you feel overwhelmed, try developing a system. Collect all of the brochures and information packets you've accumulated since your college hunt began. Divide them into categories, with one pile for schools you're sure you'll apply to, one for schools that are possibilities, and one for outright rejections.

The first round of rejections should be easy, as you eliminate schools that don't have programs you're interested in, are too far away, or don't appeal to you for some other reason. Place information from the schools you're most enthusiastic about in the certainties pile. To help sort the possibilities, you may want to make a list of everything you're looking for in a college and then check it against these schools. Devote more than a day to your sorting process. If you're tired from looking at a great many brochures from colleges you're not interested in, you'll be more likely to dismiss schools that are genuine possibilities.

When you first start out, your possibilities pile may be larger than either of the other two. Ultimately, you'll want to eliminate this pile, with all of the schools categorized as certainties or rejections. By the time you've finished this phase, the number of schools you want to apply to may be greater than you imagined.

Chances are, you'll want to apply to more than one college, but avoid overextending yourself by applying to too many. You may lose your focus if you apply to a large number of schools. This could lead to subpar essays, rushed letters of recommendation, and incomplete answers on your forms. College applications are expensive, as well. Most schools charge a fee for applying, to be sent in with the completed application forms. Fees generally range anywhere from twenty to one hundred dollars, with some schools charging even more and a few charging less. These fees can quickly add up.

To reduce time spent applying to colleges, you should look into the Common Application. The Common Application is a college admission application that students can use to apply to more than three hundred colleges and universities. By using the Common Application, you can cut down on the busywork of filling out the same basic information—like name, address, courses taken, and SAT/ACT scores—on multiple college applications. You can submit the Common Application to schools either via print or online. To get a full picture of you as an individual, some schools that accept the Common Application will request that you also submit additional information, often called supplements. These supplements can range from a few yes/no questions to several full essays.

The Common Application for Undergraduate College Admission is one way to provide an admission application online or in print to multiple colleges using the same application. Visit the Web site https://www.commonapp.org to find out more.

Balancing Your Choices

The final cuts you make to the list of schools you want to apply to are often the most difficult. If you have trouble deciding which potential schools to drop from your list, you may want to set a firm limit on the number of schools you apply to and stick to it. Take a long, hard look at the advantages and disadvantages of each school. Even if you've had your heart set on a school from the very beginning of your search, you may find that it doesn't fit your needs.

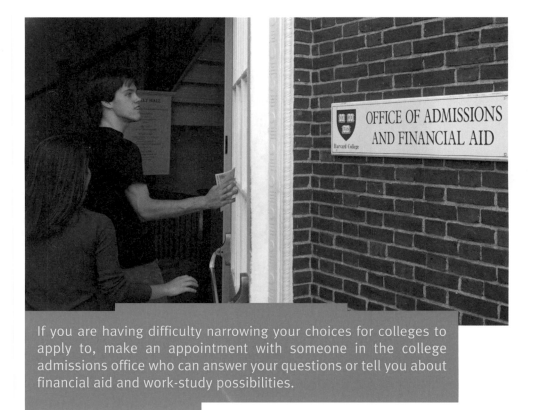

If you are having difficulty narrowing your choices for colleges to apply to, make an appointment with someone in the college admissions office who can answer your questions or tell you about financial aid and work-study possibilities.

Don't be afraid to include elite colleges that may seem like long shots, but keep the list balanced. Schools generally publish the percentage of applicants that they accept each year. The greater the percentage, the higher your chance is of being admitted. These high-acceptance schools are often informally referred to as safety schools, especially by applicants who appear more highly qualified than most. Include schools that you feel you have a good chance of getting into, as well as a few backup safety schools. If you don't gain admission to your top choices, there's still a very good chance that you'll get into one of your safety schools. Remember that you can always apply to transfer to another college if you keep your grades up and don't get discouraged. There's also a chance that you'll fall in love with your safety school, finding opportunities there that you would have missed at any of your top choices.

Early Admissions

If there's a particular school that you really want to attend and feel that you have a good chance of getting into, you might consider applying for early admissions. Early admissions deadlines often arrive in November of your senior year, so you have to have everything ready months in advance of most college admissions deadlines. You also have to be absolutely certain that you want to go to that particular school. If you are accepted for early admission, you'll probably have to make an early commitment to attending that school. This allows the school to calculate how many open places it'll have for new students applying during the regular application cycle.

Early admissions can have advantages. By applying for an early decision, you'll be taking yourself out of a much larger pool of applicants in favor of a smaller set with slightly better odds. You'll know the college's decision in December, when many of your classmates are still putting together their application materials. If you're accepted, you'll be relieved of the tension of not knowing. You'll be spared from writing several more application essays, filling out more admissions forms, and soliciting letters of recommendation for additional schools.

Applying for early admissions can help to ease the tension of not knowing which school you'll attend after high school. The college may still require you to send in your senior grades before you can register for classes.

There are also disadvantages to applying for early admissions. You won't have nearly as much time to prepare your application materials as you would for regular admissions. You'll also be cutting your senior grades from consideration, as well as any increases to your grade point average, class rank, or SAT and ACT scores. There's the chance that the college will either deny you admittance or defer its decision until the regular admissions cycle. This can leave you scrambling to put together applications to other schools at the last minute. Be sure to carefully weigh both the positives and negatives before applying for early admissions.

Ten Great Questions to Ask

1 What schools interest me the most, and why?

2 Is a four-year college right for me, or should I go to a two-year college instead?

3 Should I apply to a large school or a small one?

4 How far from home am I willing to go for college?

5 How many schools do I want to apply to?

6 What field of study interests me the most?

7 Will serving an internship or apprenticeship help me to decide on a future career path?

8 Should I apply for early admissions?

9 Who should I ask to write letters of recommendation for me?

10 How much time should I spend writing my essays?

WHAT IS THE APPLICATION PROCESS?

The application process itself may vary from college to college and may even be different for multiple programs within the same school. Most schools, however, ask you to provide the same type of information. If you're applying to a number of schools, draw up a schedule to help you manage deadlines. Set up your own deadlines for handling each part of each application.

Typically, you'll be asked to send in a completed application form, letters of recommendation, transcripts of your high school course work and grades, and a short essay. If you are applying to enter a performing arts program, you'll probably have to set up an audition. For visual arts or creative writing, you'll need to put together a portfolio of your work to demonstrate your abilities. You will also have to arrange for your SAT or ACT scores to be sent to the school by the College Board, the company that administers the tests. Some schools may ask for a face-to-face interview, for which you'll have to prepare.

Forms and Interviews

You'll probably want your parents or guardian on hand to provide vital information when you're filling out application forms. Many forms closely resemble each other and ask for basic background information such as your date of birth, what schools you've attended, your citizenship status, and what jobs you've held. These forms become easier to fill out after you've completed your first one, since you have that information at hand.

If the school requires an interview, you will likely meet with people within the admissions office and within the college administration. Interviews are most common for early admission applicants and for students applying for specific scholarships. The interview will likely be scheduled well in advance, probably during a period when all of the school's applicants are being interviewed. Your interviewers may ask you to tell them about yourself, your academic background, your interests, and your goals. Take these interviews seriously and be prepared because the people you meet with are taking time out of their schedules to give you this opportunity.

Standardized Tests

For most college applications, you will probably have to take a standardized test such as the SAT or the ACT. These tests are

Completing the paperwork that colleges require during the application process can be challenging. Most colleges ask that prospective students take the ACT or SAT standardized tests for college admission.

designed to measure how much you've learned in mathematics, vocabulary, and composition, with your scores reflecting your knowledge and abilities. Most high school students take the SAT or ACT in their junior year, though some may take it earlier. Many students also take the PSAT, a scaled-down version of the actual SAT test, which is designed to familiarize them with the format and give them an indication on how well they may do on the actual test.

The importance placed on the scores from these tests differs from school to school. Some don't require standardized tests at all. Many students take these tests multiple times, hoping to improve their scores. There are probably classes available in your area that help you prepare for standardized tests. Institutions such as trade schools or art schools may place more importance on work experience or portfolios.

Letters of Recommendation

College applications usually ask you to provide letters of recommendation. These letters are typically written by people outside of your immediate family who have the authority to speak on your behalf and outline your qualifications for attending a particular school. These letters are usually meant to be confidential and are seldom seen by the applicant. This allows the writers to express themselves freely as they discuss the applicant's qualifications. Schools often provide cover forms for the writers to fill out and require that the letters arrive in sealed envelopes.

Some schools require that all letters come from your teachers or guidance counselors, while others do not make any specifications. The best letters often come from people who know you well. Teachers, guidance counselors, coaches, employers, and community leaders are all excellent people to ask for letters. Ask well in advance of your application deadline to give them time to write and refine the letter. Many schools ask for more than one letter. If you're applying to more than one school, you may not want to ask the same people to write on your behalf for each program. Remember to thank them for their trouble after they hand you the sealed envelope containing the letter.

Essay Questions

Many colleges require that you write at least one essay—generally less than five hundred words—on a particular topic as part of your application. Over the course of your high school career, you've probably written dozens of essays on any number of subjects. Still, writing an essay for your college application can be the most intimidating part of the entire process. While the essays you write for your classes are often specific to a given topic in a particular subject, like science or history, admissions essay questions are designed to generate a broad range of responses. They typically ask you to answer based on your own experiences, beliefs, or impressions.

Schools often use the essay responses to differentiate between similarly qualified candidates. Unlike other parts of the application, the essay allows you the chance to impress the admissions officials with your personality and your writing style. Take time with your essay. Start it weeks in advance of the application deadline. When you have a rough draft, go over it carefully, making revisions to adjust your grammar, tone, and structure. Ask others to read and critique your essay. If you're stuck on a particular point, friends or family members may have useful suggestions. Your teachers will likely be happy to proof-read for grammatical or spelling errors, as well as go over the essay's general tone and structure.

Remember that you'll probably have more than one essay to write. Try not to spend so much time perfecting an essay for one school that you neglect the others. If you're applying for

Colleges frequently ask that you write an essay on a specific topic to submit with your college application. Make sure you polish your writing and that you proofread your essay before you send it in.

scholarships, you'll probably have to write additional essays, often on a choice of topics. Vocational or professional schools may not require an essay but will probably place greater importance on interviews, recommendations, and perhaps a demonstration of skill.

All of your applications will likely be complete by the end of winter of your senior year. Acceptance letters will start coming in sometime in early or mid- spring. This time, you'll get to choose which offer of admission you want to accept. Will it be the college you dreamed of before the application process began, or one you discovered as you narrowed down your choices? Perhaps you'll choose the large university located in your hometown, or maybe you'll pack your bags for the culinary institute several states over. Any one of those choices could be the right school for you.

SIX

HOW DO I PURSUE A CAREER IN THE MILITARY?

While going straight to college might be the best thing for many high school graduates, it isn't the only option. Many young men and women leave high school to pursue a career with the U.S. military. Whatever your talents or interests might be, a career in the military can prepare you for what you want to do in life. It can also give you the opportunity to travel, learn valuable job skills, and meet a variety of interesting people.

Many people make a lifelong career in the military, but this is not necessarily for everyone. If you don't think a lifelong military career is for you, you may choose to join the military for a few years, and then leave for a civilian job. Enlisting in the military is a good way for you to discover what you are good at. You can sign up for two, three, four, or more years, and then take the knowledge you have learned with you into the civilian world.

Of course, enlisting in the military is a very serious decision, especially during times of conflict. You could literally be asked to put your life at risk.

General Facts About the Military

Before addressing the steps you need to take when joining a branch of the military, it might help to know more about military careers in general. When joining the military, enlistees sign a contract. The military agrees to provide you with a steady job, wages, benefits, and training in any of a large number of occupations. In return, the enlistee agrees to serve for a specified period of time, which is called a service obligation. The standard service obligation—which may differ from one branch of the military to the other—is approximately eight years. Enlistees must serve at least two years on active duty, or full-time military duty. The rest of the contract may be fulfilled in the reserves. It's also important to know that, in wartime, you may even be required to serve beyond the time of your original obligation.

The pay scale in the military, set by the U.S. Congress, is the same in all branches. All enlistees earn a monthly salary upon entering the service and earn cost-of-living increases every year that they serve. In addition, food, clothing, and shelter are provided. Incentive pay is given to enlistees engaged in special or hazardous work, such as parachute jumping and explosives demolition.

This senior master sergeant is a personnel superintendent in the U.S. Air Force. A career in the military can be a lifelong one. You can also serve two or more years and take your training, learning, and life experiences to the civilian world.

Military compensation includes benefits and bonuses, medical and dental care, vacation time (one month for every year you serve), free legal assistance, recreational programs, and retirement plans. It also offers an opportunity for education after your service has ended. Upon signing the Montgomery GI Bill (MGIB), you contribute a portion of your monthly salary for twelve months. In return, if you are eligible, the MGIB provides up to thirty-six months of education benefits toward a college education or other vocational or job training after you complete active duty.

The military is the largest employer in the nation. Nearly 1.5 million active-duty individuals are employed by the five branches of the military at any given time. The military offers more than two thousand enlisted job specialties, which are divided into the following twelve broad categories: human services; media and public affairs; health care; engineering, science, and technology; administration; service; vehicle and machinery mechanic; electronics and electrical equipment repair; construction; machine operator and precision work; transportation and material handling; and combat specialty. Training in any of these fields can help you develop skills that you can also use in a civilian job once you leave the military.

Get the Facts First

It cannot be stressed enough: you should give enlistment into the military careful consideration because this is a decision that will shape your life.

It's especially useful to talk to at least one or two people who have served in the military about their experiences. The recruiting office you work with will be able to share information and even refer you to others. But you may not get an objective opinion. Remember, it's the officer's job to recruit people to join the military. To get several perspectives, see if you have any family members who have served and could talk to you. Your parents may know people, or perhaps some of your friends have older siblings. Your school guidance office may also be able to give you names of former students who joined the military.

If you decide to pursue a career in the armed forces, a recruiting officer at a recruiting station can provide you with military career information and enlistment options, requirements, and procedures.

You should also research the military in your library and on the Internet. Look at the material that the government provides, and perhaps look at material from some groups that are critical of the military. You may not agree with either side 100 percent, but it may help you get a sense of the pros and cons of joining the military.

Finally, discuss the decision to join the military with your parents, caregiver, or other trusted adult. This is a huge decision to make, just as is the one for attending a four-year or two-year college, and you'll want to talk it over with the people closest to you.

The Enlistment Process

You can enlist in the armed services as early as age seventeen. Although you do not necessarily have to have a high school diploma, military representatives will tell you that it is preferred.

If you decide to enlist, there are several steps you will need to follow to finalize your entrance into the service. The first step is to talk to a recruiting officer. Recruiting officers are available to the public to give information and advice about enlisting. They will inform you about training opportunities and qualification requirements. They will also schedule enlistment processing for you if they see no potential difficulties that may stand in your way (health problems, for example). You should trust your local recruiter to help you decide what is best for your future in the armed services. That is what they are there for.

However, you should never feel pressured to join the military by an enthusiastic recruiter. It is wise to talk to your parents and even a guidance counselor before you make a decision. You need to realize that if you do make the decision to enlist, there is a real chance that you will be deployed to fight in a war. Sometimes, recruiters can be overly enthusiastic and pressure you to make a decision, often without ever realizing it. Never feel as though you need to decide right away. Always take the time you need to think it over.

Also, don't feel pressured to join the military because you think that it's your only choice or it seems an easy option. Military careers can be very rewarding, but they are almost never easy. Remember: you always have choices, and you should never join because you feel it is your only option.

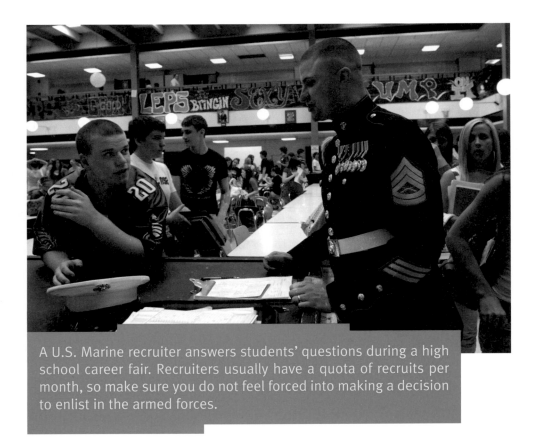

A U.S. Marine recruiter answers students' questions during a high school career fair. Recruiters usually have a quota of recruits per month, so make sure you do not feel forced into making a decision to enlist in the armed forces.

To enlist, you must qualify for enlistment. At this time, applicants must go to a military entrance processing station (MEPS) to take the Armed Services Vocational Aptitude Battery (ASVAB), which helps determine if applicants qualify for military service and, if so, what jobs they qualify for. The ASVAB includes nine individual tests in the following subjects: word knowledge, paragraph comprehension, arithmetic reasoning, mathematics knowledge, general science, auto and shop information, mechanical comprehension, electronics information, and assembling objects. ASVAB scores are good for two years, and the test can be taken in high school in preparation for enlistment. Applicants will also receive a medical exam. Then, applicants will meet with a service classifier. A service classifier is a military career information specialist. By entering your aptitude scores into a computer that matches them with your interests, the service classifier will figure out which positions are best for you. Then, you select an occupation and schedule an enlistment date. Before finalizing this step, you must sign a contract with the branch of your choice, and take the Military Oath of Enlistment, which is the same for all the branches. The last step in the enlistment process is promptly going to your assigned base for basic training.

Basic Training

The purpose of basic training (which lasts between six and eleven weeks) is to mentally and physically prepare new enlistees for service in the armed forces. Not only will you be required to undergo rigorous physical training, you will also be required to attend and pass classes with subjects relating to your experience in the military. You will be trained in such areas as weapons use, first aid, and map reading, just to name a few. Basic training for the five branches of the military differs. The base at which an enlistee trains depends on the job training he or she is to receive. Recruits are divided into groups of forty to eighty people. Soon after these groups are formed, they meet with their drill instructors, receive uniforms and supplies, and move into their assigned quarters.

Daily exercises are designed to improve conditioning, stamina, and overall fitness. Although physical conditioning is a major focus during basic training, building a sense of pride and discipline is equally important. When basic training is completed, enlistees move on to job training, which often takes place in another location.

Reserve Officers Training Corps (ROTC)

If you are torn between attending college and enlisting in a branch of the military, the Reserve Officers Training Corps, or ROTC, might be the answer for you. This program is an elective course offered at many colleges and universities around the country, and it's staffed by active-duty personnel. ROTC is the single greatest supplier of officers to the armed forces today, in both active and reserve duty. The army, navy, and air force each run separate ROTC programs. Regular and reserve officers for the Marine Corps come from the navy ROTC program.

ROTC enrollees learn leadership and management skills while actively participating in training schedules similar to those in the military. Sometimes, this means spending your Saturday mornings running or doing calisthenics. Of course, ROTC students are also enrolled full-time in college. Being involved in an ROTC program means being strongly involved in hands-on training for an officer position in the armed forces.

A typical ROTC program takes four years to complete and is designed to fit with a standard college class load. You can enroll in two years of ROTC training without being obligated to join the armed services upon graduation. Students interested in an

Reserve Officers Training Corps (ROTC) cadets from a Michigan university compete in a rope event during an army training program. The ROTC is an elective course at colleges and universities that helps train students to become officers in the armed forces.

ROTC program will encounter a mixture of classroom time and hands-on experience.

Branches of the Military

The five branches of the U.S. armed services—the army, the navy, the air force, the marines, and the coast guard—each offer many career opportunities for young enlistees, not to mention competitive wages and promotion prospects. Deciding which branch is best for you might be difficult. However, once you have properly researched your options, you should be able to make a well-informed decision.

Give It Some Thought

Perhaps one of the five branches—the U.S. Army, Navy, Air Force, Marine Corps, or Coast Guard—could be the right choice for you. Be smart and take the time to investigate your options by asking the people close to you what they think you should do. But don't stop there. Stop in and talk to recruiters representing a few different branches about your options.

Being a member of one of the five branches of the military means being committed to serving your nation in times of war and peace. It means making a promise to your fellow Americans to defend them, their property, and their liberty when called upon to do so. The armed services have much more to offer enlistees than a chance to become adept soldiers. Young men and women in the military are guaranteed solid, hands-on training—provided they work hard and strive to do their best.

Becoming an Officer

Many military personnel make the decision to become full-time soldiers instead of accepting an honorable discharge from the armed forces when their active or reserve duties have been completed. Becoming an officer is a career path in and of itself, and it can result in a lifetime of fulfillment, not to mention the attractive benefits that are offered.

To become an officer in any of the five military branches, an individual must meet certain criteria. All branches require that the applicant be a high school graduate, pass a medical and physical exam, and be at least seventeen years old. In addition, to be considered for an officer position, an applicant needs to work toward or already have obtained a four-year college degree. If college is not in your future plans, becoming an officer may not be the right choice for you. If you do intend to earn an undergraduate degree, you may be a good candidate for officer status. The ROTC is another path that you may decide to follow to become an officer in the armed forces.

As a student graduating from high school, you have numerous options to consider for pursuing your education and career training. Whether you decide to attend a college, trade school, vocational program, or training in the U.S. armed forces, the decision is yours to make. Once you know what it is that you want to achieve, have explored your options, gathered the information, weighed the pros and cons, considered the consequences, and thought it through, you will be able to make the choice that is right for you.

administration Referring to the individuals involved in the management of an institution or business.

apprenticeship An arrangement whereby a person learns a job or trade while working for someone already skilled in the area.

campus The grounds on which the buildings of a college or university are situated.

curriculum An integrated course of academic studies.

dorm A college or university building containing living quarters for students.

elite Selected as the best.

extracurricular Outside the regular academic curriculum.

faculty The body of teachers and administrators at a school.

hierarchical Classified according to various criteria into successive levels or layers.

intern A student who works for little or no pay to gain experience in his or her chosen field.

letters of recommendation Letters written by teachers, coaches, counselors, or people you have worked or volunteered with, which describe your good qualities and strengths.

portfolio A body of professional work, such as paintings, drawings, photographs, videos, films, etc.

recruiter In college admissions, a person associated with a school who is designated to answer questions and hand out information at college fairs and other events. In the military, a recruiter gives information to the public about enlistment into the armed services, training opportunities, and qualifications.

reference A formal recommendation by a former employer to a potential future employer describing a person's qualifications and dependability.

reserves There are two types of duty in the armed forces. The first type is active duty, which means that you are considered a full-time soldier. The second type is reserve duty, which means that you are a part-time soldier and that you attend training only one weekend every month, plus two full weeks per year.

scholarship Financial aid provided to a student on the basis of academic merit.

vocational Relating to a vocation or occupation; especially providing or undergoing training in special skills.

For More
Information

Army ROTC
(800) 872-7782
Web site: http://www.goarmy.com/rotc
  The Web page provides information about the ROTC
  training and curriculum, career paths, scholarships, and
  cadet and officer profiles.

The College Board
Headquarters
5 Columbus Avenue
New York, NY 10023-6917
(866) 630-9305
Web site: http://www.collegeboard.com
  This company administers the SAT, the ACT, and other
  standardized tests. Its Web site features practices, tests,
  and advice on preparing for the test, as well as online
  test registration. It also provides information on planning,
  finding, applying, and paying for college.

College View Careers and Majors
c/o Hobsons
50 E-Business Way, Suite 300
Cincinnati, OH 45241
(800) 891-8531

Web site: http://www.collegeview.com/careers/index.html
  The Web site offers advice on how to select a major and
  choose a career path.

eCampus Tours
c/o Edsouth
P.O. Box 36014
Knoxville, TN 37930-6014
(865) 342-0670
Web site: http://www.ecampustours.com
  A Web site that allows users to research schools and look for
  scholarships. It features advice regarding college planning.

FinAid Page, LLC
P.O. Box 2056
Cranberry Township, PA 16066-1056
(724) 538-4500
Web site: http://www.finaid.org
  This company and its Web site provide student financial aid
  information and feature tools and advice to help estimate a
  family's estimated contribution.

Ministry of Training, Colleges and Universities
Public Inquiries Unit
880 Bay Street
Toronto, ON M7A 1N3
Canada
In Ontario: (800) 387-5514; outside ON: (416) 325-2929

Web site: http://www.edu.gov.on.ca/eng/general/postsec/
    college.html
    This Canadian organization provides information about col-
    leges of applied arts and technology in Ontario. It includes
    material about finding and choosing a college, admission
    requirements, cost, college life, and job possibilities.

Quintessential Careers
1250 Valley View Lane
DeLand, FL 32720
(386) 740-8872
Web site: http://www.quintcareers.com/teens.html
    The most popular career site for teens on the Web,
    Quintessential Careers offers advice for planning a career
    as well as resources such as job-hunting tools and a resume
    service.

U.S. Army
Web site: http://www.army.mil
    This is the official home page of the U.S. Army.

U.S. Coast Guard
Web site: http://www.uscg.mil
    This is the official home page of the U.S. Coast Guard.

U.S. Department of Education
400 Maryland Avenue SW
Washington, DC 20202
(800) 872-5327

Web site: http://www.ed.gov/students/landing.jhtml
This department of the federal government offers information about student aid; planning for college; finding colleges based on location, programs, tuition, distance learning, and evening courses; and information about career colleges and technical schools.

U.S. Marine Corps
Web site: http://www.marines.com
This is the official home page of the U.S. Marines.

U.S. Navy
Web site: http://www.navy.mil
This is the official home page of the U.S. Navy.

Web Sites

Due to the changing nature of Internet links, Rosen Publishing has developed an online list of Web sites related to the subject of this book. This site is updated regularly. Please use this link to access the list:

http://www.rosenlinks.com/faq/cact

For Further Reading

Bachel, Beverly K. *What Do You Really Want? How to Set a Goal and Go for It! A Guide for Teens*. Minneapolis, MN: Free Spirit Publishing, 2001.

Bolles, Richard Nelson, Carol Christen, and Jean M. Blomquiest. *What Color Is Your Parachute for Teens: Discovering Yourself, Defining Your Future*. Berkeley, CA: Ten Speed Press, 2006.

Bravo, Dario, and Carol Whiteley. *The Internship Advantage: Get Real-World Job Experience to Launch Your Career*. New York, NY: Prentice Hall Press, 2005.

Bruno, Franklin. *Armed Forces*. New York, NY: Continuum, 2005.

Cohen, Katherine. *The Truth About Getting In: A Top College Advisor Tells You Everything You Need to Know*. New York, NY: Hyperion, 2002.

Fiske Edward B. *Fiske Guide to Colleges 2007*. Naperville, IL: Sourcebooks, Inc., 2006.

Fiske, Edward B., and Bruce G. Hammond. *What to Do When for College: A Student and Parent's Guide to Deadlines, Planning and the Last Two Years of High School*. Naperville, IL: Sourcebooks, Inc., 2007.

Garcia, Cara L. *Too Scared to Learn: Overcoming Academic Anxiety*. Thousand Oaks, CA: Corwin Press, 2002.

Greene, Howard, and Matthew Green. *Making It into a Top College: 10 Steps to Gaining Admission to Selective Colleges and Universities.* New York, NY: Cliff Street Books, 2000.

Hernández, Michele A., ed. *Acing the College Application: How to Maximize Your Chances for Admission to the College of Your Choice.* New York, NY: Ballantine Books, 2002.

Johnson, Spencer. *Who Moved My Cheese for Teens.* New York, NY: G. P. Putnam's Sons, 2002.

Mitchell, Joyce Slayton. *Winning the Heart of the College Admissions Dean: An Expert's Advice for Getting into College.* Berkeley, CA: Ten Speed Press, 2001.

Paradis, Adrian A. *Opportunities in Military Careers.* New York, NY: McGraw Hill, 2006.

U.S. Department of Labor. *Young Person's Occupational Outlook Handbook.* Indianapolis, IN: Jist Works, 2000.

U.S. News Ultimate College Guide 2008. Naperville, IL: Sourcebooks, Inc., 2007.

Webster, Jeanne. *If You Could Be Anything, What Would You Be? A Teen's Guide to Mapping Out the Future.* Clayton, GA: Dupuis North Publishing, 2004.

Yale Daily News Staff. *The Insider's Guide to the Colleges, 2008: Students on Campus Tell You What You Really Want to Know.* 34th ed. New York, NY: St. Martin's Griffin, 2007.

Index

About the Author

Jason Porterfield has written numerous books for young adults on subjects ranging from American history to job training to environmental science. He earned a B.A. degree from Oberlin College and has completed his graduate coursework in journalism from Columbia College Chicago. He resides in Chicago, Illinois.

Photo Credits

Cover © www.istockphoto.com/Chris Schmidt; p. 6 © Tony Savino/ The Image Works; p. 7 © www.istockphoto.com/Michael Madsen; p. 9 © www.istockphoto.com/dra_schwartz; p. 12 Shutterstock.com; pp. 14, 25 © Jeff Greenberg/The Image Works; p. 16 © Robert West/ *Dallas Morning News*/Newscom; pp. 21, 28 © Kathy McLaughlin/ The Image Works; p. 23 © Bob Daemmrich/The Image Works; p. 31 © Glen Cooper/Getty Images; p. 33 © James Marshall/The Image Works; p. 38 © www.istockphoto.com/Pattie Steib; p. 41 © www. istockphoto.com/Sean Locke; p. 44 U.S. Air Force; p. 46 © Don Emmert/AFP/Getty Images; p. 48 © Mary Knox Merrill/*Christian Science Monitor*/Getty Images; p. 51 Staff Sgt. Russell Lee Klika/ U.S. Army.

Designer: Evelyn Horovicz; Photo Researcher: Amy Feinberg